T0064047

Solitary
Reflections

Solitary Reflections

SAILEE BRAHME

PARTRIDGE

To order additional copies of this book, contact
Partridge India
000 800 10062 62
orders.india@partridgepublishing.com

www.partridgepublishing.com/india

Introduction

'Solitary Reflections' is a compilation of the poems penned down over the last decade. These poems are on varied subjects that have been close to or touched my heart and soul. They have often been the result of a flow of words and tears in abundance, while a few have catapulted from the thoughts deeply ingrained in my mind for years. The poems reflect the emotions and ideas that I have felt passionately about or the worries that have plagued me.

I believe all of us come up with questions but seek no answers. This book will give everyone a chance to mull over things that are very obvious as well as to take notice of all that is mundane or taken for granted.

Acknowledgements

My dream of pursuing writing has been encouraged and nurtured by my parents since many years and I shall always appreciate the support they have given me. I thank all my close friends who have been the inspiration behind so many poems in this book and who have also helped me edit and revise my writing from time to time by providing thoughtful criticism. I extend my heartfelt gratitude to all the teachers who have blessed me with the language skills that I put to use every day. They appreciated my efforts, motivated me to write and to publish my poetry. The list of people who have a share in my success would be incomplete without my pet dog, who has been my constant companion on this journey of writing that I began some years ago.

Contents

People

Life

Nature

Love

1. The Moon

The moon is full and shining bright

I'm right here, soaking in her light.

I'm drenched in her glory,
     her light caresses my face

I feel peaceful

Thoughts disappear at a glacial pace

I feel the breeze in the trees, on the water
     and in my hair

I don't know who is around or why

And neither do I care.

I bask in the beauty of the moon,
     feel the power of Nature

That seems condescending

Making you feel so small in stature.

She inspires awe, she exudes pride

I just gaze at her

With a blank paper by my side.

2. A Dream

She is grace when she walks

She is poise when she stands

She is a fragile treasure

As she gives her hand in your hands

She is beautiful in silence

She is striking in speech

Gliding to her destination

Eager to reach

She is poetry in motion

She is solid in resolve

A raw stone on the river-bed

A diamond waiting to evolve

She is dazzling in her smile

She is music in laughter

Somebody's inspiration

Somebody's happily ever after

She is honesty in anger

She is strength in tears

A comfort in embrace

A whisper in the ears

The twinkle in her eye

And you are smitten

A tale of irrevocable love

Waiting to be written!

3. Bundle of Joy

A hat bobbing on her curls,

Ribbons flying with the wind,

She trotted up the path

Wearing a pretty smile;

She picked flowers with her tiny hands,

And filled the cane basket,

She wandered over the hill

For more than a mile.

She jumped over rivulets,

Collected blue and green pebbles,

And counted the sparrows that flew by;

She made flower garlands and

Wore them like a crown,

Stared at ladybugs and honeybees

As she lay under the endless sky.

She pointed to clouds that looked like animals,

Hopped and jumped over anthills,

Rolled down the grass slope

Giggling all the way;

She lost a shoe,

Stepped into puddles,

Her face shining like the sun in May.

I watched Sara from the cottage door,

A picture of happiness

Even without a toy;

And with every passing moment,

Her delight warmed my heart

As I watched my daughter-my joy !

4. Wrecked

Feel so broken

Feel so torn

Lost in time

Lonely and forlorn.

A smile that never reaches the eyes.

A heart that yearns for something and sighs.

Fingers that clutch emptiness

Hoping for a hug or just a caress.

Someone else resides in me now

She bleeds my spirit out.

I belong to everybody

With neither protest nor a shout.

They can do what they please

But I'll be here.

Writhing in pain

Pleading with fear!

Wiping salt off my cheek

I line my eyes with Kohl

Knowing nobody notices them

Sure they won't see my damaged soul.

I walk in the rain

Wishing the scars would fade

But what's the use?

New will soon be made!

5. Saviour

Save me from the fire

Save me from the flood

Save me from the distress

Save me from the blood

Take me away from treachery

Take me away from lies

Take me away from betrayal

Take me away from the wise

Let me tumble

Let me run loose

Let me go wild

Let me find my muse

Hold me when I fall

Push me when I stall

Pick me when I fail

Help me set sail

A way to go far

A journey to that lone star

A place to call our own

A heaven that will be Home.

6. My Shadow

You once said to me- 'Oh, it's just a dog!'

And I cried for hours.

It's not just a dog.

He is a part of me, maybe much deeper
     than you will ever be.

I know it's not right to compare.

And anyways, he's incomparable to a human.

He is so much greater.

The most loyal being one can ever find.

He is not selfish.

He never breaks his promise.

He loves me unconditionally at all times.

I can act as though he doesn't exist,

And still be sure that he will never leave me.

The look in his eyes says that no one in the world
is more important to him than me.

He will be there for me; with me;

To the fullest of his capacities.

I will never have cause to doubt him.

He is my shadow.

Wherever I go; he goes too.

We will be together till our last breath.

And I'm sure after that too.

7. Without Me

I won't be in your arms

But I'll linger on your mind.

I won't see you as you come home

But my fragrance you will find.

We won't watch the sunrise together

Nor the starlit sky

But when at the beach you sit

Our memories will pass you by.

When you look into the mirror

I'll be right behind you

Don't think I've left you alone

Remember I love you too.

I wish I could change fate

And spare you the grief

But I was suffering dear

Withering away like a leaf.

I couldn't let you know

I couldn't see you weep

Our loss is physical

But the pain goes deep.

You are my strength, my purpose, my joy, my life

And I know I'm your faith, your pride;
    not just your wife.

I didn't want to let go

But I didn't have a say

Time went by so fast

And all I wanted was 1 more day.

We woke up together

But I did not see the dawn.

Now I may not be around, but life must go on!

Promise me you won't give up

Continue the journey without me

If I know you're alright

Peaceful even in death, I shall be !

8. Silence

The beauty of silence is seldom appreciated.

A person is so accustomed to sound,
    that silence seems out of place.

Maybe that's how the metaphor
    – 'awkward silence' came up.

But silence is the beholder of infinite power, love,
        care, forgiveness, acceptance,
        friendship and humanity.

Silence speaks so much more than
        words can ever express.

It conveys what is needed; effortlessly.

It gives you the power to deny; conveys comfort
        and shows love in the purest form.

A firm handshake, a warm hug,

    a shoulder for support;

Are a language seen by the blind,

    heard by the deaf,

    and spoken by the mute.

It is through these gestures that we can cross

    any language barriers;

No matter where we go,

No matter whom we meet.

9. The Journey

Looking at a bunch of roses, I thought-

Our life is like this flower.

Tiny and timid at the beginning,
      sheltered in a bud,
      protected from harm.

Slowly, the bud blooms.

Our world opens and grows
      like the blooming flower.

Our life connects with other lives.

The blooming continues…

Our world widens.

Acquaintances increase.

We are always surrounded by people.

Always ready to share things.

Always ready to help.

The flower is in full bloom now-
everything is going great.

Then, the petals start drying.

They turn black.

One by one, they fall.

People too, get distanced.

The crowd surrounding us decreases.

We try very hard, but we cannot go against the
rules of nature.

The drying and falling of petals
cannot be stopped.

Loss; cannot be avoided.

But the flower is not sad.

It has fulfilled its destiny.

It has given joy to someone.

It has conveyed someone's feelings.

It has shown love.

It has apologized.

It has congratulated.

As life goes on, we experience the same.

And like the flower, we are never disheartened.

We have lived life to the fullest.

We have made a difference to the world.

Tomorrow, there will be another rosebud.

Awaiting its turn to bloom.

10. Faith

Once I sat at the window,

    looking out over the ocean.

The wind seemed like it was talking to me.

I watched the waves come rolling in

    and dash against the rocks near the shore,

    almost a hundred times.

The rocks were huge. Solid. Immovable.

The waves had force but were not strong enough.

The rocks seemed to me- a cold hearted cynic

    who does not believe that

    the world holds anything good;

Who does not believe that people can be selfless,

    helping, kind or plain human.

The waves were- the goodness that resides in the
   heart of every person.

The waves knocked on the door
   to the cynic's heart every 15seconds.
   But he refused to let the goodwill in.

I ignored this new, bizarre idea that had suddenly
   occurred to me and looked away.

A month later, sitting by the window again, the
   idea returned.

I looked at the rocks carefully and was stunned.

The relentless efforts of the waves
   had eaten away at the rocks
   causing some to dislodge,
   some to crumble away
   and most to become very smooth.

That's when I realized that goodness can penetrate
   every rock, every heart, and every soul.

You cannot refrain it, however much you try.

We may not respond appropriately,

> but the good that has to happen,
> will happen.

People will perform charity.

A stranger will help you in need.

And you will be forced to accept;

That in a world rampant with vice,

Humanity will prevail.

11. My Best Friend

I find writing incredible.

It feels wonderful to have
 a means of expressing yourself.

The joy of writing cannot be put into words.

I write about so many things-
 people, nature, music, life.

It's as though I'm trying to explain to people
 how I perceive things.

Through free verse, I can express
 my deepest thoughts.

I am not bound by any rules of writing
 or grammar of the language.

What binds me to my poetry is the love of
 reliving what I once felt.

It does seem strange though,

    reading what you created years ago.

But sometimes; words just don't come.

Poetry does not flow.

It is alarming. It is fearful.

What once came naturally does not any more.

The mind is blank and so is the paper.

No thoughts to pen down.

Nothing to describe.

Nothing to complain about.

Nothing to envy.

Nothing to love.

Fear sets in.

Am I unable to think?

Have I lost my perception?

Do I no longer have people around me
    to write about?

And then I suddenly realize;

I'm still writing.

I'm writing about myself.

There is someone who can never desert me.

As long as I have myself, I'll never be alone.

The words will go on…..

And the poetry will flow….

12. Patience

My violin looked beautiful.

The wood- polished, shining.

The bow- firm and straight.

The pegs- well and tight.
    Tuned to the perfect note.

Ready to help me create a harmonious melody.

I start with a few notes; they sound beautiful.

Hymning an old song, I try playing it.

The tune flows from my mind and heart,
    right onto the strings.

It's as though the notes knew
    I wanted them to be heard.

I get engrossed in my music.

I'm playing it flawlessly;

The bow is running firm on the strings;

My fingers are falling on the right notes and the
music seems like a gift to the ears.

I'm too engrossed.

The tempo of the song increases.

Fast.

My fingers dance on the strings.

Faster.

The bow is running back and forth.

Faster still.

Suddenly, I cut my finger on a string.

The music is interrupted by a disturbing silence.

I notice the fibers of the bow have got loose.

I try the next string and unexpectedly; it breaks.

I am speechless.

One moment, everything was going great.

Now, everything's going wrong and I can't stop it.

The entire beauty is lost. I have to stop.

I'm hurt and so is my violin.

Many times in life-

Everything is just going perfect.

Suddenly, nothing seems right.

Everything goes haywire.

We feel lost.

We know, eventually, it will all be right,

But it will take time.

The finger will take time to heal;

The string will have to be replaced;

The bow will have to be repaired.

But; it all needs time.

That wait is something we cannot bear.

We are restless. Time is longer than ever.

We are disheartened.

We lose hope. We refuse to try.

And the violin gets packed into its case
    and put on the loft;

Never to be played again.

If only I had given it sometime;

If only I had changed the string
and repaired the bow;

My music would have continued.

If only I had waited…

13. Regret

They scar you forever.

They eat you from within.

They turn into wounds that
> even time can't bring a soothing.

They bring floods of tears.

They inflict unending pain.

They make the mind restless and you feel insane.

They make you want to scream.

They leave an empty space in your heart.

They become your nightmares
    and never seem to stay apart.

They render you helpless

People call them Regrets.

I call them an Abyss!

14. Tears

When tears flow,

It is liberation.

It is relief.

Peace. Solace. Silence.

Destroyed in anger.

Broken in pain.

Feeling incomplete.

Or ecstatic.

Self-realisation and judgements.

Accusations or betrayals.

Layers of unexplainable emotions.

But let them flow;

Coz there are things for which

language doesn't suffice.

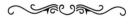

15. Giving

Our teacher once told us a story.

'It is said, that God watches us all the time.

He loves us and wants us to be happy.

When we pray to him, or ask for something,

he showers us with blessings.'

'But'- she said, 'he will always bless us sparingly-

like the water that remains

at the bottom of a glass

even after it has been emptied.

The blessings he showers upon us-

water from the glass.

And the water that remains at the bottom-

blessings that he withholds.

He gives happily.

But he never gives everything.

Because he wants us to keep going back to him.

If we got everything that we asked for,
    we wouldn't give him a second thought.

He doesn't want to let that happen.'

That story remained in my mind
    for the next many years.

And I thought- Don't we all act that way?

We are expected to give. But we don't give our all.

We crave for attention.

We want people to come back to us too.

Whether we teach, give, share or explain,
    it is always 99%.

The last 1% ensures and secures
    our superiority over others.

It helps to establish that we have something
that others don't.

So next time when we expect 100% from someone,

We will remember this story.

16. Birth of a Poem

Where does a Poem rise from?

It takes birth deep inside,
    at the bottom of the heart.

A few roots extend into the stomach too.

The branches fan out
    into my veins, muscles, arteries.

Leaves grow intro the throat, the ears,
    the fingers even.

Some want to reach the mind.

The Poem travels upwards.

Sometimes it gets a little lost behind the eyes.

A little flows away with tears.

But the journey is complete when

Leaves surround the mind.

The tree is in full bloom

And finally,

Fingers dance on paper.

17. Utopia

I was travelling in a crowded bus at 7 pm,

But nobody even accidentally pushed
or touched me.

I got off and started walking.

Took a lonely path but I did not keep glancing
over my shoulder.

A group of men came from the opposite direction

But my muscles did not tense.

I did not find the need to hold on to my bag or
adjust my clothing.

I walked carefree

Not having to lower my eyes or slouch.

I sat on the street bench looking for my cell

When a stranger approached,

    asked if I needed help

    and also offered me his phone.

"May I drop you home? "He asked.

And a million unsafe thoughts

    did not rush into my head.

I did not have to worry about men

    lurking in the shadows

Or about how I was dressed.

He picked up another friend on the way.

Not once did I wonder-

    "where are they taking me?"

He dropped me home

Without any inquisitive questions.

"Thank you so very much."

"Oh not a problem. Hope you find your phone. Good bye."

And that was it.

Just some sincere help from a fellow citizen.

Although only in an ideal world,

I did feel safe for one evening.

18. Be a Kid

Jump around on the bed.

Sing loudly all of a sudden.

Put on loud music and dance.

Be a kid.

Make a mess.

Throw tantrums.

Be annoyingly stubborn.

Be a kid.

Soil your clothes.

Pick up stray animals.

Get paint all over yourself.

Be a kid.

Cry openly.

Howl for chocolates.

Forget your table manners.

Be a kid.

Don't be reserved.

Forget poise and grace.

Be innocent.

Remain a kid.

19. The Battle

The mind said to the heart,

'Don't you have any sense?'

The heart asked,

'Don't you have any feelings?'

The mind told the heart,

'Come with me. You'll never go wrong.'

The heart replied,

'Come with me. You'll learn from experience.'

The mind said- 'You get hurt'.

The heart replied- 'You get confused'.

The mind said- 'You're too honest'.

The heart said - 'You lie too much'.

The mind said- 'I decide.'

The heart said- 'Your actions.'

- 'I judge.'

- 'Your decisions.'

- 'It all starts with me.'

- 'It ends with me.'

- 'I'm superior. I can break.'

- 'I only mend.'

- 'I can rule the world.'

- 'Without me, there wouldn't be anyone to rule over.'

Thus went on, the clash between the mind and
the heart;

And the mind began a fierce competition,

While the winner watched in silence.

20. My Devotion

It flows in my blood,

It courses through my veins,

It burns in my heart,

It runs in my mind.

It lives in my breath,

It rings in my ears,

It sings in my voice,

It is one of a kind.

It resides in my eyes,

It loves in my dreams,

It hates in my world,

It beats in my soul.

It falls in my tears,

It smiles in my laughter,

It becomes more than passion,

It forgets it's role.

It is my prayer,

It is my devotion,

It sets me free,

It takes me into a trance.

It is purer than water,

It is stronger than stone,

It is truer than the sun,

It is my dance.

A reason to live

A calling to follow

A sincere duty

The magic of beauty.

21. Madness

There is always a bit of madness,

In Dreams.

They turn you into a believer.

There is madness

In Love.

It turns you into a rebel.

There is madness

In Art.

It creates a painter.

There is madness

In Joy.

It makes you dance.

There is madness

In Sorrow.

It makes a writer.

There is madness

In Children.

They turn you into a child.

There is madness in everything.

If only we would embrace it...

But then,

Nobody wants to go Mad!

22. Hope

They say; Love makes the world go around.

I feel it is Hope that makes the world go around.

Even with the most positive attitude,
    we know we can't have it all.

But we still hope.

Hope is the only thing that prevails –

Over science, reality, common sense and logic.

Even when all these tell us –

'No, it won't happen';

Hope whispers –

'It might!'

Hope governs our life.

A farmer hopes for rains.

A soldier hopes for peace.

An orphan hopes for a home.

A player hopes for a win.

I hope for Hope.

Because if that's what makes the world go around;

We are going to need a lot of it.

23. Priceless

Nostalgia and memories

Dreams and reveries

Hope that never dies

Joy overflowing from the eyes

A kiss from a child

A stroll in the wild

Putting flowers in your daughter's braid

Assuring your son that bruises and scars will fade.

Learning bird calls and whistles

Making giant soap bubbles

Counting colors of the rainbow

A big bonfire and hot cocoa.

Vivacity and empathy

Enthusiasm and compatibility

Purity of thought and peace of mind

Perseverance and faith of every kind

A healthy body, a beating heart

A meaningful life till you depart

You may be rich

You may want to give it a try

But there are some things money just can't buy.

24. The Farmer's Sorrow

He sat in a corner of his field.

His gaze was turned towards the sky.

Every day he would come out onto his field and
walk over the cracked earth.

He dreamt of how once,
his field had been lush green;

The way his children were always eager for the
sowing and the reaping;

How his bullocks helped him dig the soil
during the rains.

But now; there were no rains;

No bullocks;

No grains

And no more family.

His wife and children hadn't eaten for days.

He remembered the night they slept
    and never woke up again.

His palm caressed the parched earth;

He looked up at the clouds again.

But the only water that fell onto the soil was,

His tears.

25. Apocalypse

We've read that the Earth is in agony.

She's in pain. She is being destroyed.

She's crying out for help.

But don't you see?

She's past that stage.

She's silent.

She's still.

The silence is creeping up slow and vicious.

It's the calm before a storm.

She's waiting.

Waiting to take revenge.

Waiting for the point where man's sins
    will finally tip the balance.

And then she will rise.

She will tear apart the ground
    and feed you to fire.

She will lash out with the water from the sky.

She will uproot everything man ever built.

She's been docile for such a long time
    while man continued exploiting her.

Now she waits,
    with fiery eyes and destructive arms.

She will render everything barren.

She will rule.

Man will suffer.

She will torture.

Man will plead.

She will destroy.

Man will perish.

26. In the Heart of the Ocean

As deep as the Ocean,

We always say

She holds so many secrets

That go into her every day.

Gems and jewels

Or sailors lost at sea,

A letter in a bottle

Or a lock and key.

Debris from flooded cities

Or gallons of oil,

Fishermen and their nets

or acres of soil.

She bears curses

For separating lovers.

She witnesses goodbyes

From teary-eyed travelers.

She feels the pangs of families

That fail to survive her waves.

She looks on helpless

As men dig each other's graves.

She watches the glaciers melt into her

And sewage dumped in the water;

As man loses more land every day

And the planet becomes hotter.

27. Colour

Life would be incomplete without Colour!

The Ocean wouldn't be so beautiful,

If the sky wasn't blue to be reflected.

Monsoons wouldn't be pleasant,

If there weren't a million shades of green
    all around.

A candle wouldn't create a soft ambience,

If its flame wasn't a fiery yellow.

Would food be so tempting
    if fruits and vegetables were colourless?

We wouldn't watch the sun set,

If it did not turn the horizon an orange golden.

The world would be empty without Colour!

We wouldn't exist if it wasn't for

The bright white moon,

The red blood,

The brown soil

Or the inexplicable colours of our skins, eyes and

our hearts.

28. The Healer

Have you ever pondered over the power of music?

Did you ever realize the effect it has on us?

It can convey celebration.

It can make us weep.

It can instill fear in our hearts.

It can soothe.

It is a means of life.

Part of the journey.

It can mend.

It can heal.

It can calm.

But it can break as well.

It brings together people of all kinds.

It gives company to a lone person.

Music kills internal differences.

It's like a magnet that attracts people.

Music has the power to undo all the lines;

    that have been drawn by man;

On the basis of language or colour.

29. In Love with the World

I learnt French
  and fell in love with the Eiffel tower

I learnt making Pasta and fell in love with Rome

I learnt belly-dance and fell in love with Arabic

I learnt Spanish architecture
  and fell in love with Art

I learnt history and fell in love with India

I learnt philosophy and fell in love with Greece.

I learnt Hockey and fell in love with Canada

I learnt weaving Kimonos
  and fell in love with Japan

I learnt to distil vodka and fell in love with Russia

I learnt to salsa and fell in love with Cuba

I learnt making tortillas
    and fell in love with Mexico

I learnt to wear a Burqa and fell in love with Iran.

I learnt to eat dates and fell in love with Dubai

I learnt soccer and fell in love with America

I learnt to plant tulips
    and fell in love with Amsterdam

I learnt to play the bagpipes
    and fell in love with Scotland

I learnt KungFu and fell in love with China

I learnt something from every culture

I learnt something from every country

But I didn't just learn;

I realised I've fallen in love with the world.

30. La Vie En Rose

Just being in love brings a smile to my face

Lifts my spirits and

Mystifies my grace.

I live for myself no more

I'm lost to the world

And belong to him like never before.

I feel a presence around me

He is a part of every action

I weave my life according to him

And make him the sole subject of affection.

Even if it was one sided

I'd gladly take the fall.

Coz it's better to have loved and lost

Than to have never loved at all.

31. Caring

I'll be the mirror, in your moments of doubt.

I'll be the path, when you feel lost.

I'll be the shoulder, when tears well up.

I'll be the air, when you feel suffocated.

I'll be the tree, when you need shade.

I'll be the souvenir, so that memories never fade.

I'll be the sky, when you want to feel free.

I'll be the ocean, when you need a sunset.

I'll always be there, coz I know life isn't fair.

I'll always be there, coz I care!

32. Rare Beloved

A four leafed clover

A fallen star

A diamond in the river

A black rose

A mermaid on the rocks

Snowfall in the desert

Once a month sunrise

An eclipse

I counted the rare and unique-

That leave you speechless.

But the list was incomplete without you-

My beloved.

33. Exchange

The twinkle of stars

I'll take from your eyes

The light of the moon

I'll take from your heart

The bright sunshine

I'll take from your smile

The softness of petals

I'll take from your hands

The peace of the mountains

I'll take from your embrace

The flow of water

I'll take from your words

The music of the ocean

I'll take from your laughter

The zest of life

I'll take from your breath

The touch of feathers

I'll take from your lips

The comfort of a home

I'll take from your voice

Myself-I'll take from you!

34. Fragrance

That fragrance-

It soothes my tears

It calms my fears

A smile it brings

And gives me wings

It takes me high

It lets me fly

Envelopes me

Brings me close

Tender and sweet

Just like your rose

Decorates my dream

Makes you seem

Like my permanent sunshine

Smooth as old wine

Makes my heart flutter in an instance

Your presence, your aura, your fragrance!

35. The Wait

Every night I lay in bed

A small part of me refuses to sleep

Waiting for a missing part

My heart that is yours to keep.

Count the hours where you are

Away from my touch or eyes

Crave for the distance to melt

And tell myself no lies.

That you miss me too

That you will be back

That you will complete us

And all that we lack.

I hear just my breathing

But two beating hearts

Use the million tears

To join the broken parts.

I hide under the quilt

In the pillow I bury my head

Ask my mind to relive

All the memories instead.

Now I hear just my own heart

I find no more the other

My breathing becomes slow too

And all I do is shudder.

36. Helpless

I want to write for you

But I don't know what.

How can I pen down

How you are in my every thought

My heart is full of you

And so is my head

I'd rather my arms be full instead

Why should I miss you so much

I don't own you

I took many efforts to stop

Successful ones are very few

I feel incomplete in bed

I feel incomplete when I rise

I wish you were all mine

And all this was just lies

Wish you were here

Not in a far off land

So we could stare at the stars

And lay in the sand

Come back soon

I feel lost

I know you're doing your duty

But at what cost

You know it's a waste

You know it's not right

Leave the darkness behind

Come into the light

Let my arms guide you

To a place where we are free

To jump in the water

Or even climb a tree

Rock me to sleep each night

Watch the sun rise on my face

Of your past worries

We won't keep a single trace

I love you and

I want to be there

Give me a chance to feel loved

Please try to be fair

I didn't feel distance

Would harm my heart

We had spoken

I knew from the start

But you didn't leave alone

You took a part of me

And though I want to be whole again

Nothing can let me be

I can't stop smiling when

I think about you

But then my eyes get moist

And tears flow too

But I've decided to stop

Questioning myself

I know my love is strong

You know I have faith in you

I've done nothing wrong

So I will wait

Even though I feel clueless

Coz my belief might falter

But my love is helpless !

37. Unfair Love

A long time had passed

I didn't belong to him

He wasn't mine either

It was years since I'd seen him last.

But that sultry summer evening

Our paths crossed

Or should I say

We found something

We had actually never lost.

A sudden thunderstorm had lashed out

And he struggled with his umbrella.

That silhouette I'd recognize anywhere

There was not a hint of doubt.

I stood rooted to the ground

Wondering what was going to happen.

Would he walk away or

Would he turn around?

I was getting drenched but I didn't care

He took cover outside a shop
        and took off his jacket

I just imagined what I could dare.

At last he saw me

The only one standing in the street

He too must have wondered whether to approach

Or let me be.

The rain hid the tears streaming down my cheek

But I saw a ray of sunshine

The smile that

Made me go weak.

A moment of recognition and time stood still.

Our story had run its course

And I didn't know if I could muster the will.

I took a deep breath and stepped forward

Your face lit up

Your eyes gave away your anxiety

I felt like a flightless bird.

A hand caught my wrist

I turned but stared ahead

"Where are you going?"

He whispered and kissed.

His eyes followed my gaze

He saw me looking at you

He stared back at me

And I saw his eyebrow raise.

"Let's go; you're soaked."

His grip tightened.

I tried to find words

But my heart only hoped.

He led me away

But I left something there

An emptiness, a yearning

A love unfair.

38. Soulmate

She was vivacious

He was mature

She was childish

He was responsible

She was the shore

He was the sand

She was the tree

He was the shade

She was the candle

He was the flame

She was the fire

He was the heat

She was the water

He was the tranquillity

She was the mirror

He was the reflection

She was the soul

He was the mate.

39. I Can Fly

As long as you trust me, I fight the world.
As long as you handle every situation,
I make mistakes.

As long as you support me,
I undertake impossible tasks.

As long as you are around, I breathe.

As long as you love me, my heart beats.

As long as you sigh next to me, I sleep peacefully.

As long as you hold our child, my eyes overflow.

As long as you infuse our life with songs, I dance.

As long as you provide me with the clays of joy,
I sculpt our life.

As long as you bring home vigour,

    I decorate the sculpture with excitement.

As long as you give me the emotions,

    I write the poetry.

As long as you sow the relations,

    I nurture our home.

As long as you confide in me,

    I become your friend.

As long as you give me wings, I fly.

40. Immortal Love

The urge to create a symphony with words

For my loved one

Knocks on my door every night

I rush to let her in

To make of her a string of pearls

Or the young one of a bird in flight

Can words be exhausted?

Or thoughts be mundane

With overuse?

The picture paints itself

The sculpture comes to life

Only for the Muse.

Poetry has flown for generations

And surely shall not perish

Just when my muse beckons me

Beethoven and Napoleon wrote love letters

But even better will a young woman write today

The world will see.

If love is eternal

How can lovers die?

It's just an earthly notion

Amour, Amor, Amore,

No language needed

Only unadulterated devotion

Your lord is different

So is mine

But they are equally jealous

We have ignored their importance

It is our affection and faith in each other

That makes them anxious.

The All-Seer won't believe his eyes

He will not accept his mind

When his legacy is rendered mortal

By the fondness of our kind.

Printed in the United States
By Bookmasters